Marxism and Political Correctness

Donald H Sullivan

ISBN: 978-1-329-38110-0

~~*~~

The Politically Correct Movement

The Politically Correct (PC) movement is Marxist in origin. It is not new. It started with Karl Marx's *The Communist Manifesto* (1848) and his *Das Kapital* (1867-1894.) These works are considered the start of the Marxist Socialist movement.

Marxism, or Communism, kicked around for a long time in Europe before it finally caught on in Russia in 1917. The movement strengthened in Russia but stalled there. Later it attempted to gain a foothold in Germany. The German Marxists started *The Institute of Social Research* in Germany, but when they were beginning to make significant gains, Hitler came to power.

Hitler's own socialist movement, the *Nationalist Socialist Party* (Nazis,) saw the institute as a rival and shut them down. Most of the members fled to America and established the Institute of Socialist Research in the U.S.

The Marxist movement was slow to catch on in the U.S. They reorganized as the Communist Party USA (CPUSA,) and then founded worker's unions, their slogan being "Workers arise, you have nothing to lose but your chains." Later the Unions broke away from the Communist Party.

The CPUSA gained a firmer foothold when some of the professors from the Socialist Institute of Research managed to infiltrate a number of American universities. At that point in time we were worried about the rise of Nazism, and Communism was not yet considered a threat to our way of life in the U.S.

Hitler and Stalin were vying for leadership of the socialist movement, but agreed to a non-aggression pact to avoid armed hostilities. The pact ended with Hitler's invasion of Russia. After Hitler's defeat in World War II, Stalin became the sole leader of the socialist movement. However, Mao Tse Tung's victory over the Nationalist Chinese in 1949 gave him the power to rival Stalin's leadership.

Having professors in U.S. colleges spreading Marxist propaganda has been a boon to the PC movement. College students are at an age where they are most impressionable, and so they are susceptible to the brainwashing of Marxists. Part of the brainwashing of these young people includes convincing them that what they are being fed is not Marxism or Communism, but benevolent socialist ideals.

The Marxist movement slowed down with the advent of The Cold War between the western powers and the Communist Bloc...mainly the Soviet Union and Red China. However it began to spread rapidly during the sixties among the leftist anti-war activists during the Vietnam War. It quickly became a Liberal cause, and Marxism was firmly established. Political correctness of the Left has become an effective tool of the Marxists, with leftist Liberals also using it to the max.

The fall of the Soviet Union had no effect whatsoever on the Marxist movement in the U.S.

~~*~

Most people think of the PC movement as something that just spontaneously happened, with no leaders or no guiding principles. Almost everyone thinks that the ideas of Political Correctness are nonsense, such as punishing a first grade boy for telling a girl she's pretty, or punishing another for drawing the likeness of a pistol.

In Virginia Beach, VA, a child was playing with a toy gun in his own yard while waiting for the school bus. The kid was suspended from school for a year for playing with a *toy gun*. Just one of countless examples of the PC movement gone wild...to the extent that it boggles the mind.

Most of us will be outraged about such things, say it's stupid, and then forget it the next day. None of us stop to think that this is brainwashing, or thought control, starting at a very early age. The thought control builds up as the student moves through high school and on into college (not all high schools and colleges, thank goodness, but far too many.) All but those who are strong willed and intelligent enough to see through the PC propaganda come out of college thoroughly brainwashed.

The term "PC police" has come into vogue, but is generally thought of as a joke. We think there is no such thing as a real PC policeman. But the PC police are a reality. Who are these PC police? They are the teachers and professors who punish their students for saying or doing something that is not politically correct.

The PC Police are government agencies who conduct sensitivity classes on how to be politically correct. They teach them what to say, how to act, and how to think. Employees can expect to be punished if they do not adhere to the PC principles. Sensitivity classes are simply the equivalent of the Communist retraining camps.

Many of those who act as PC police do not even realize that they are supporting the cause of Marxism. They have been duped into believing that what they are doing is virtuous.

Employees, not only in government agencies, but also in the private sector, have been castigated or even fired for things like having a confederate flag on a lunchbox, wearing a cross that is visible, or for uttering certain taboo words. In pre-PC days individuals who were offended by such actions would have been considered as oversensitive petulant crybabies. If the offense was serious enough they would have either sued for slander, or met the offending individual after work and settled the score.

Some believe that the idea of PC is to keep from offending people. Trouble is, PC itself is offensive to a great many people. For those of you who don't remember what it was like in the pre-PC days, there was something far better than PC that kept people from offending others. Courtesy, politeness and respect for others kept us pretty well behaved toward each other.

There were rude and impolite people in those days to be sure, but they were a very small minority, and people seldom got ostracized or fired for being impolite. The big difference between PC and common courtesy is common sense. PC is almost totally lacking in both common sense and reason.

Americans have always been a generous, compassionate people. The average everyday American is actually far more generous and compassionate toward fellow human beings than those who adhere to Marxism and political correctness. They profess to side with the poor and downtrodden, but look at every country that has fallen to

Marxism and their citizens are far poorer and more oppressed and downtrodden than capitalist countries like the U.S.A.

It's always the people of Marxist controlled countries trying to escape and come into capitalist countries, never the other way around.

But to the Marxists, common sense and reason are not important. What is right and what is wrong are not important. Whether or not something is offensive is not important. *What is important is the conditioning of people on how to think or how to act. Mind control.* They will be punished for saying or doing anything that is not politically correct. People must be brainwashed enough so that they are afraid of saying or of doing the wrong thing, and once this is instilled in people we have mind control. And this is the end result of political correctness.

Already this is happening in America. Large numbers of us are being manipulated by the Marxists. We say and do as they tell us through the tyranny of the PC movement. We've been conditioned to believe that political correctness protects minority groups, and that if we resist or even hint at resisting, we fear we'll be branded as racists, homophobes, or Islamophobes.

Other PC police are private employers, the entertainment industry, and the media. Many people in the media and entertainment business have been victimized by the PC police. Howard Cosell, Don Imus, Hank Williams, Jr., Paula Deen, Jimmy "The Greek" Snyder, and "Tuffy" Gesling, (the Missouri rodeo clown,) Tim Tebow, and Donald Trump, just to name a few. Those named here are just some of the celebrities, the list of non-celebrities is much longer.

In pre PC days these people might have been mildly berated or asked to apologize. It might have been mentioned in a paragraph in the back pages of a newspaper. But people were rarely , if ever, fired because of personal arguments or insults.

Football fans will remember Howard Cosell as a sports announcer on Monday Night Football. His transgression? As he watched a smaller than average black ball carrier racing down the field, he said to his fellow announcer, Don Meredith, "Wow. Look at that little monkey go."   In pre PC days such a remark would have gone unnoticed.

That's a common expression--a term of endearment, really-- that can be heard in everyday conversation fairly often. It could as well have been "little rascal," "little bugger," "little sucker," as well as "little monkey." Howard Cosell had a good reputation, never having made a racial comment during his career. He was well known for his good relations with Muhammad Ali. He came across as a little on the arrogant side, but was generally liked when teamed up with down-to earth Don Meredith.

Don Imus lost his job because of making a comment about The Rutgers women's basketball team, joking that they looked like "nappy headed ho's," *a term made up by black hip hop artists*.

Hank Williams Jr, known for his song "are you ready for some football?" at the beginning of *Monday Night Football*, compared a game of golf between Obama and John Boehner to Hitler playing golf with Benjamin Netanyahu.   He explained it was like polar opposites playing together.   He made the comparison on "Fox and Friends," during an interview. Some thought he was comparing Obama to Hitler.   Though Williams has denied this, he was fired from Monday Night Football. Good old PC in action.

Paula Deen confessed that she had used the "N" word early in her life, and that got her fired from her cooking show. The PC police will not accept that people can change throughout their lives...some bad to good and some good to bad. Nope, the PCM is unforgiving.

Jimmy "the Greek" Snyder, another sports announcer, once speculated that Blacks were good athletes because their ancestors were bred to be strong by their slave owners. This got him fired. The fact is that, on the whole, black athletes are better than whites, and what the heck, don't we all have ideas or theories as to why things are as they are?

Tim Tebow openly declared himself to be a Christian, and as a result teams won't sign this excellent quarterback for fear of being branded as politically incorrect. (Note: At   this   writing   the

Philadelphia Eagles have signed him up, after a one year absence from football.)

Donald Trump offended illegal Mexican immigrants by saying that many of them are criminals and riffraff, which some of them are. Trump was merely telling it like it is, which in itself can get you in trouble with the PC police.

The PC police lumps all Hispanics together, whether they are legal or illegal, and no matter their country of origin. It doesn't even matter if they are second, third, or fourth generation Americans, they are lumped together with those who entered illegally. Anyone who speaks against illegal immigrants is, in the eyes of the Marxists, guilty of insulting all Hispanics.

Tuffy Gesling, a rodeo clown, wore an Obama mask during a Missouri rodeo contest, and believe it or not, he was fired for this. PC gone wild. A rodeo clown once wore a Bush mask and nothing happened except people thought it was funny...which is the way it should be. After all, this is a free country, at least it has been until lately.

The rodeo clown incident is just another example of how the PC movement is trampling on our Bill of Rights. Most all politicians have jumped on the PC bandwagon condemning Mr. Gesling for daring to wear the Obama mask. Mr. Gesling was exercising his right of free speech and is being punished for it. This should make all Americans boiling mad. Once we lose our precious right of free speech, it will affect us all. It is a giant step toward tyranny.

One of the main reasons that our ancestors fled England was to escape persecution because of criticizing leaders. And here we are, *allowing the PC movement to subject us to the very same oppression that we fled.*

Free speech and dissent should not be stifled, it should be encouraged.

When it is pointed out that other presidents have been ridiculed in all manner of ways, the PC crowd says it is different with Obama. It is *not* different with Obama. He is our president...all the people's president, no worse or no better than any president before him. And like all presidents before him, he is fair game for criticism and ridicule.

Some say that the clown's choice of costume was in bad taste, but even if that were so, it was no crime or no reason to punish the clown. Some may think it was in poor taste, but taste is subjective. Others may see nothing but harmless humor, as has been the case with mocking other presidents.

As long as we adhere to our constitution, none of our leaders will be treated like royalty.

If Mr. Gesling had been arrested, as was called for by the PC-minded NAACP, any of us could be arrested for merely expressing our views or criticizing any politician once the precedent has been set. Now it is a rodeo clown, tomorrow it can be political cartoons and shows like SNL. If a future president thinks the NAACP is offensive to him, he could have its leaders arrested. The NAACP should think this through before making any such demands. This can be a two edged sword.

~~*~~

Since the PC movement has permeated our culture, we can no longer tell jokes about each other. In days past, Italians, Poles, Mexicans, Irish, and other groups told jokes about each other and laughed together. There were radio and TV shows like *Life With Luigi*, about Italian immigrants; and *Amos n' Andy*, about Blacks. No one complained until the advent of the PC movement, and then such shows were pulled.

Note that this is not to say that all these groups were one big happy family. There were sometimes fights between some of the groups. An old joke pretty much sums it up: A guy stands on a soap box and says, "All of us gathered here today are now at peace with each other, with no more fighting and hard feelings among the Italians, Poles, Puerto Ricans, and others here. Now that we're all together, let's go beat hell out of them damn Irish Micks."

Oddly, *Amos n' Andy* was replaced by *Sanford and Son*, a PC blessed show that showed Blacks in a much more offensive way than *Amos n' Andy* did. Both shows were funny, but many thought *Amos n' Andy* was the funnier of the two. Anyone watching it knew it wasn't intended to degrade Blacks in any way. The show was farcical, and not intended to be realistic, as were other farcical shows like *Green Acres* or *The Beverly Hillbillies*. It would take an extremely thin skinned person to be offended by shows like these.

~~*~~

The Spread of the PC Movement

In the fifties, political correctness was exclusively about Blacks. Hispanics, Asians, and Gays were unobtrusively in the background. Muslims were unheard of. In the fifties, Muslims were members of a religion that was foreign to Americans, there was but a very small number of them in the U.S., and in this country, at that time, they were thought of as an obscure religious sect.

Hispanics and Asians were generally accepted. In the military services Blacks were segregated but Hispanics and Asians were not. Also, in the days before PC there were no military regulations in regards to a soldier being a homosexual. There were regulations against soldiers performing homosexual acts, but regulations also forbade heterosexual acts as well.

Gays have generally been accepted into American society. Most people have no heartburn with the gay lifestyle. But some oppose gay marriages, though such marriages are approved by the PC movement. The opposition comes mainly from religious groups, but there are those who feel that it is just not right or natural for people of the same sex to marry. Others consider it just plain silly that two people of the same sex would marry, something comedian's joked about a few years ago.

Although Hispanics have always been accepted into American society, and have gotten along fairly well with "Anglos," in the last few decades the PC movement has driven a wedge between the two groups. The PC movement declared it politically correct to support illegal immigrants

They then proceeded to lump legals and illegals together, with the idea of making all Hispanics feel as if they are unwelcome in America. This is effectively driving a wedge between Anglos and Hispanics.

The PC police have designated *all* Hispanics as an oppressed group and many legals have been brainwashed into thinking that the majority of Americans consider them the same as illegals.

~~*~~

Marxists, with their PC movement, have divided us. What better way to subdue an enemy than to divide and conquer? Their ultimate aim is to eliminate capitalism and establish socialism. With runaway welfare already with us and socialized medicine just around the corner, we're well on the way to becoming a socialist nation.

The America that the people of the world loved, and came here from countries all around the world by the millions looking for the freedom and promise of the good life that America offered is no more. The "shining city on the hill," as President Reagan once described it no longer makes good on the promise of freedom. The descendants of the Americans that immigrated here and made this country great have let it slip away from them, all because they failed to recognize the PC movement for what it was: a movement created by Marxism to divide us and control our thoughts.

~~*~~

One of the greatest achievements of the PC movement has been the rules they established for the raising of our children. Parents no longer have the right to raise their children as they see fit. A spanking on the child's rear end, once considered the customary way to discipline errant kids, is now considered to be cruelty, punishable by law.

A simple spanking was no more than using a paddle or bare hand on the child's rear end. It wasn't brutal, as would be a heavy stick that could injure the child, or a horsewhip that could draw blood. At worse, a parent might use a limber switch from a peach or willow tree.

Many parents in bygone days didn't resort to physical punishment unless the offense was serious. A good "talking to" sometimes did the trick. Some parents let the errant kid sweat it out in some cases. They would tell the kid something like, "I don't have time now, so I'll take care of this tomorrow morning." Sometimes the kid would get a swat or two the next day, but as often as not he would get a "chewing out." But in such cases, the waiting and sweating it out was the main punishment.

A favorite saying by the PC crowd is an old African saying, "It takes a village to raise a child." That is probably true in small communities like a village. It is obvious that it would not work in heavily populated areas of developed nations. A better saying here would be "It takes a solid, morally upright family to raise a child." Many single parents have also successfully raised children.

The effects of this current lack of discipline can be seen today in misbehavior, low school grades, bullying, and disrespect for authority. Crime is rampant. Sure, we've always had a crime problem, but even in the days of Al Capone and Bonnie and Clyde it was not as widespread as it is today. Undisciplined children are more easily controlled by Marxists who have infiltrated our school system, and molded into "useful idiots" that will serve the Marxist cause.

As widespread as crime is today, the PC movement makes it even worse. Liberals decry the "deplorable" conditions of prisons if they don't have TV, dayrooms, gyms, etc. Prison inmates often have it better than military personnel. The idea of prisons is to lock up miscreants to protect the general public and to punish those convicted of a crime. We should treat them humanely, of course, but not make life pleasant for them. Many ex cons have openly stated that they wouldn't mind going back to prison. To them it's "three hots and a cot" and a fairly pleasant stay.

The PC movement is even changing history to become politically correct. Anything good or idealistic that has been done by the early European settlers in America is either glossed over or omitted, while their bad deeds have been magnified. At times even some of their great accomplishments have been painted as evil deeds.

Historical buildings such as slave markets have been deemed to be offensive to black people, and have either been demolished or designated as other types of structures. Statues and monuments of the Old Confederacy have also been deemed to be offensive, and have been demolished or hidden away.

At some point in the future people will curse us. What we now do in the name of political correctness is no different than the tyrants who have burned books that they didn't like, or Muslims destroying ancient works of art that they deemed offensive.

The old Soviet Union changed history to suit the ideals of their socialist government. At the time our media condemned them for it. Now we are guilty of doing the same thing, and the media applaud.

The PC Movement is Discriminatory

It is now politically correct to demonize Whites. Jews, once considered an oppressed minority are now grouped with the Whites. All Hispanics were once considered by the PC movement to be an oppressed group, but since the Zimmerman trial, the white Hispanics have fallen out of grace with the PC movement. Of all the Whites, only those who are Muslims are classed as an oppressed group. Liberal Whites, though not considered to be oppressed, are considered champions of the oppressed by the PC movement.

The PC Movement and "White Privilege"

Hundreds of thousands of Whites have grown up in poor families. They know what it means to have outdoor toilets and no electricity or running water. They know what it means to have shoes with flapping soles or cardboard inner soles to cover holes in their shoes, raggedy clothes, and to be ridiculed by other kids in school. They walked to school because their families couldn't afford bicycles. Meat was a rarity at meals, and treats like cakes, candy, and ice cream were extremely rare.

But the PC movement does not recognize poor Whites. Whites, according to the PC movement, are the privileged class.

Any White who tries to claim that he grew up in a poor family is immediately mocked and told by the Liberal types that he can't possibly have known poverty like Blacks knew it. It is simply politically incorrect to say you were poor if you're white. Facts are not facts unless approved by the PC movement.

If you were born white, you should be ashamed. You should feel guilt. It doesn't matter if your ancestors never owned a slave, or even if they arrived after the end of slavery, just being white makes you an accessory to those slave owners who have been dead for over one hundred and fifty years. One college professor suggested that all whites should commit mass suicide. Let's hope that he was joking.

There are many Whites and Blacks who are friends, including those in the South. They work together, party together, fish together, and pray together. There are Blacks and Whites who are Army buddies and school chums. Please note that this is not to say that all Blacks and Whites are one big happy family of friends with each other, but only that there are many who are friends. Indeed, some are close friends.

But the PC movement does not recognize that conservatives or southern Whites can have Blacks as friends. That southern Whites and Blacks can be friends does not fit the PC movement propaganda theme that southern Whites are privileged and consider Blacks as an inferior race. In the eyes of Liberals, southern whites are uninformed, slow, high school dropouts, and ignorant trailer park rednecks, while Liberals are informed, well educated, enlightened intellectuals.

So Liberals think they can make all the judgments on what is correct or incorrect, or who is privileged or not privileged. In the convoluted thinking of the Marxist PC movement, any White who says "some of my best friends are black," is branded a racist. Another stratagem to divide us.

The fact is that many Blacks and Whites are indeed friends...even in the South...but facts are not facts unless approved by the PC movement.

~~*~~

The PC Movement and Race Baiting

The PC movement goes out of its way to stir up racial turmoil however and whenever it can. The Marxists know that their chance of transforming the U.S. into a socialist country are slim as long as there is peace and racial harmony. The more turmoil and hatred they can stir up the better their chances of taking over our country. Divide and conquer.

The PC movement has dictated that gangs, criminals, and thugs who are black will not be reported as black. The news media will refuse to identify a black criminal as being black. Even many police departments will not include race in the description if the suspect is black. The Marxist PC movement is even getting to our law enforcement officers.

There is a stretch of a jogging trail in Durham, NC that goes through a black neighborhood where joggers are often attacked by black gangs. A gang of black thugs attacked and beat a white jogger nearly to death. A TV station described the criminals as "dark complected."

Some Liberals do not realize that they are aiding the Marxist cause. They will go to great lengths to point out differences between Marxism and Liberal Socialism. At best, though, Socialism is a mild form of Marxism.

The race baiters, who also may not realize that they are aiding the cause of Marxism, work overtime to sow dissension...to the delight of the Marxists. Race baiters are very opportunistic, taking advantage of every situation to agitate Blacks by crying racism. They have succeeded in brainwashing large numbers of Blacks into believing that all Whites are evil. They preach that Whites want to go back to the Jim Crow laws of the old South, and that all Whites are white supremists.

Race baiters have a vested interest in racial turmoil. It is they who will not allow Martin Luther King's dream to come true.

Fortunately there are some Blacks who have not succumbed to the brainwashing. In the South, as well as in other regions of the country, it is hard to find neighborhoods without both Blacks and Whites living in harmony with each other. Also, more and more Hispanics can be found in Southern neighborhoods. All are more concerned with working and making a living than finding fault with each other.

Blacks and Whites work, pay their bills, root for their sports teams, watch their favorite TV shows, tend their yards and gardens, attend church, talk to each other over backyard fences, and shop at places like Wal-Mart and Lowes. They're just too darn busy with living to hate each other.

I can hear a typical Liberal sarcastic remark to this talk of racial harmony. It would go something like, "Gee, but it's great to know that there is no longer a trace of racism in the South. Isn't it wonderful going through neighborhoods and seeing all the Whites, Blacks, and Hispanics smiling, hugging, and high fiving each other?"

Nope, it ain't quiet like that; it's not all complete harmony. There's disagreements and even animosity at times, *just as it would be in an all white or all black neighborhood.* But generally speaking, the mixed neighborhoods live in harmony--in spite of the hate-mongering race baiters.

~~*~~

The PC Movement and the 1st Amendment

The PC movement has nothing but contempt for the first amendment of the constitution. They don't merely ignore it, they trample all over it. The New York City Department of Education has banned fifty words. All are common words that are heard in everyday life. Children who attend schools in New York City will certainly hear those words outside the classroom. What the PC people hope to accomplish is anybody's guess.

Here are a few of the banned words:

Abuse (physical, sexual, emotional, or psychological)
Alcohol (beer and liquor), tobacco, or drugs
Celebrities
Cigarettes (and other smoking paraphernalia)
Halloween
Homelessness
Homes with swimming pools
Hunting
Occult topics (i.e. fortune-telling)
Parapsychology
Politics
Poverty
Religion
Slavery
Terrorism
Television and video games (excessive use)
Violence
War and bloodshed
Weapons (guns, knives, etc.)
Witchcraft, sorcery, etc.

More examples of political correctness gone wild. It's difficult to imagine how any of these words could offend anyone, unless, of course, one was brainwashed into believing the words to be offensive.

~~*~~

The latest instance of suppressing free speech is in Seattle, Washington. They have banned words like "brown bagging" and "citizen." To almost everybody brown bagging means bringing your lunch to work, or in some cases carrying whiskey from the liquor store in a brown paper bag.

But the PC crowd in Seattle dug up an obscure meaning of brown bagging. It seems that in times past people were judged by whether their skin color was lighter or darker than a brown paper bag. It seems far-fetched that anyone would associate skin color with brown bags in present times. But the Marxist PC M seizes every opportunity to stir up racial turmoil.

Take the word "citizen." According to the PC police that word is offensive to illegal immigrants. Apparently it is felt that when the illegals hear the word citizen they are deeply offended. One would think they would be more apt to be offended by words like "alien" or "illegal." But the convoluted thinking of the PC crowd can be puzzling to ordinary folk.

But it's really not so puzzling when you consider that the goal of the Marxist PC movement is to stir up turmoil among us, or in other words, to divide and conquer. Now by merely uttering the common words "citizen" or "brownbag," a person can be accused of being insensitive toward those who have darker skin or who are not American citizens...or they can even be accused of racism.

The PC crowd has a growing list of words that are forbidden. A cripple can no longer be called a cripple, even though that is a legitimate word that has been in use for centuries. The dark skinned people of African heritage have in the past been called Negroes, Colored people, and Darkies, all acceptable in times past. None of those words were intended to be offensive, but those words are now on the forbidden list.

Another name on the forbidden list of the PC movement is "illegal alien." You can no longer call an illegal alien an illegal alien. You can't call a bum a bum, and can't call a retarded person a retarded person. All these words and many other words that are now taboo were commonly used in the past and not considered offensive. A bum knew he was a bum, and an illegal alien knew he was an illegal alien, so you couldn't offend a man by calling him a bum if he knows he's a bum.

Now it's taboo to say "bum' or 'vagrant," and it's PC these days to say "homeless." If I were a truly homeless person, out on the streets through no fault of my own, I would be offended at hearing a bum called a homeless person.

~~*~~

Oddly, it is now politically correct to use profanity in public, which is supposedly protected by the first amendment. However, it is obvious that the first amendment was not intended to protect those who use obscene language in public, but to allow criticism of our leaders. When the constitution was written, citizens in many countries in Europe could be arrested for criticizing their leaders. The writers of the constitution meant to prevent this.

It's interesting that many of the same European countries that tyrannized their people in those times have since adopted the constitution that those early Americans crafted over two hundred years ago. In fact many countries all around the world have patterned their constitutions after America's.

We should note that people from Marxist nations tend to flee into free nations, and not the other way around. That alone should make it difficult for Marxists to indoctrinate Americans, and yet Marxists in American universities have been very successful.

If we allow the PC movement to suppress our freedom of speech, especially our freedom to criticize and poke fun at political figures, we can expect to become like Nazi Germany or the old Soviet Union, where speech was carefully monitored, and any citizen could be arrested and imprisoned for deviating from what is deemed appropriate by the State. We're getting dangerously close to that now.

~~*~~

Not Only Blacks Were Slaves

If the PC crowd of today refuses to recognize that Whites can be poor, and that poverty is solely the domain of Blacks, how will they react when they learn that Whites were once slaves...with Blacks as their slave drivers? This was true in the 18th century in New Smyrna Florida.

Slavery is deplorable. This shameful practice has been around since ancient times, with many different peoples of the world suffering under this terrible yoke. Slavery in the New World began in the Thirteen Colonies even before the United States was born. Both the British and Spanish brought slavery here. After we won the Revolutionary War and gained our independence from England, the practice of slavery continued in just about every state.

Slavers continued to go to Africa and reward the stronger African tribes for capturing members of weaker tribes and bringing them to the slavers. Also, warring tribes would capture members of an enemy tribe and sell them to the slavers. This practice continued right up to Lincoln's Emancipation Proclamation.

Everyone knows that slaves in North America were black Africans, but few know that there were a significant number of whites who were also slaves. Large numbers of indentured servants, both white and black, were brought into the colonies. Indentured servants are not slaves as such. They willingly sign a contract to work for a master for a specified number of years, with an agreement to receive their freedom and a plot of land of their own after the term of indenture is completed.

Many of these servants, both Whites and Blacks, gained their freedom and became landowners after their terms were up.

Many others, however, whites as well as blacks, became slaves. They were not only denied their land when they reached the end of their terms of indenture, but they were forced to continue to labor for their masters under armed overseers and slave drivers.

Among the white slaves, there were 1,403 who all came from the Mediterranean area, mostly from the island of Minorca (as a group they were all called Minorcans.) They all signed contracts of indenture with a Dr. Andrew Turnbull, a wealthy Englishman. The Minorcans were to work his large plantations in New Smyrna, Florida, which was then a British colony. At the end of the contract terms, Turnbull refused to honor the contracts. He used his slave drivers and armed overseers to force them to continue their labor for ten years before being freed by the British Governor of Florida.

Conditions were so horrible aboard the seven ships used to transport the Minorcans across the Atlantic that148 of them died before reaching Florida.   During the ensuing ten years of enslavement, over six hundred more died from the terrible conditions at the colony. Turnbull also kept a few African slaves at the colony who were brought down from plantations in South Carolina. The Africans claimed that conditions were far better in the South Carolina plantations than they were in the New Smyrna colony.

They labored from sunup to sundown with no days off. The Florida heat was scorching, with droves of mosquitoes. Dysentery and other diseases were always with them. They were lashed or beaten if they stopped to rest or talked back to a slave driver. Some of the women were raped. The rations were meager and the well water was muddy and warm.

As a matter of interest, some of the slave drivers who were over the Minorcans were Africans who were brought down from plantations in South Carolina. The irony here is that today a black man may accuse a white man of Minorcan heritage for having ancestors who were slavers, but it could well be the opposite: that same black man's ancestors could possibly have been a slave driver over the white man's Minorcan ancestors. The African slaves in the colonies were in the majority to be sure, but the Africans did not have a monopoly on suffering from slavery.

The descendants of those Minorcans are pretty much spread around the country, but the vast majority can be found in the cities and towns of northeast Florida. Most are in St. Augustine with significant populations in Mayport and New Smyrna. The 1,403 Minorcans were not the only white people to be enslaved by any means, but they were by far the largest single group.

~~*~~

It has been said by Liberals...and by some Blacks, too...that only Whites can be racists. The Marxist PC movement will never acknowledge black racism, no matter how blatantly obvious it may be. Any Black who dares to tell it like it is and to recognize that some Blacks are racists is immediately branded an "Uncle Tom." *Mind control.* You must think the same way the rest of your kind thinks or they will ostracize you.

~~*~~

The Silence of the PC Movement

In Washington, DC, three black men assaulted and mauled a white man. The PC movement, exemplified by the mainstream media, Liberals, and black leaders, was silent.

In Florida, black teens attacked a white student on a bus. The PC movement was silent

In Brunswick, GA, a mother, Sherry west, was pushing her baby carriage when she was robbed by two Blacks. When she explained that she had no money, one of them shot her baby in the face. The PC movement was silent.

In St. Paul, MN, a mob of Blacks pummeled Ray Widstrand, a white Liberal who believed that living in a black neighborhood was not unsafe. He was left in a coma. The PC movement was silent.

In the eyes of the PC movement when a White attacks a Black the White is usually considered a racist and is charged with a hate crime, where a Black who attacks a White is justified in doing so because of the injustices of the bygone era of Jim Crow laws or some such.

Even events are influenced by the PC movement. On 9/11/13 two million bikers rode their motorcycles into Washington, DC as a counter protest against the million Muslim march on DC. The Muslim march never materialized, but the biker protest did...in spades. The government and the media, most probably at the behest of the government, never whispered a word about this huge, newsworthy event.

~~*~~

The PC Movement and Militant Islam

On September 11, 2001, Militant Islamists hijacked three commercial airliners full of innocent passengers and flew them into the twin towers of the World Trade Center, the Pentagon, and but for the actions of the passengers, they would have flown into the Capitol Dome or The White House.

The entire country was galvanized and united in a way not seen since Pearl Harbor. Democrats, Republicans, Blacks, Whites, Liberals, and Conservatives were all behind their president and their country. But President Bush proceeded to make a couple of dumb mistakes.

First, he told all Americans not to worry and to go on about their business. They did, and soon all but forgot the 9/11 attack. This contrasted with President Roosevelt's reaction right after Pearl Harbor. He made stirring speeches encouraging Americans to mobilize and to be ready to make many sacrifices for their country. Americans responded in a grand style...*they became The Greatest Generation.*

Had Bush rallied the American people we might have had another generation as great as *The Greatest Generation.* The mindset of Americans right after 9/11 was similar to the American mindset after Pearl Harbor, but Bush did not capitalize on that mindset as Roosevelt did. Indeed, if Roosevelt had handled Pearl Harbor as Bush handled 9/11, the Imperial Japanese would likely have conquered the U.S. with little effort.

Americans, who were fired up right after the 9/11 attack were now in the business as usual mode. This opened the door for the PC movement. The Marxists immediately went to work propagandizing the public, painting Islam as an innocent and peaceful doctrine.

~~*~~

Right after 9/11, even the liberal news media showed Muslims in countries of the Mid-East dancing in the streets and celebrating when the twin towers were brought down. Americans who initially saw them as the enemy and a threat to our way of life were slowly being brainwashed into believing *all* Muslims are an oppressed group. It was now becoming politically incorrect to criticize Islam, even the militants among them.

Liberals, who adhere to the PC movement, go so far as to claim that the Muslims who commit terrorist acts are not really Muslims. They hold that Islam is a religion of peace and that true Muslims are incapable of performing terrorist acts.

Another favorite ploy of Liberals is to bring up the Oklahoma City bombing as evidence that Christians are also terrorists. None of the three men convicted in the case claimed to be Christians. The men were anti-government activists; their motive for the act was not religious in any way.

~~*~~

Hate Crimes

The PC movement has succeeded in getting our legislators to make "hate crime" laws. Before the hate crime laws came into being, criminals convicted of crimes such as murder, rape, and assault were generally all sentenced to the same type of punishment, varying with the recommendation of the jury and decision of the judge.

Now, however, if those same crimes are determined to be hate crimes, the criminal receives a much stiffer sentence. This is another capitulation to the PC movement that is totally lacking in common sense. By the reckoning of the PC crowd, if one man kills another for reasons of racism, he must be tried and convicted of a hate crime.

Is he worse than a man who rapes and kills a ninety year old woman? Is he worse than a man who beats an eighty-nine year old war veteran to death? Is he worse than a man who shoots a baby in its carriage? Is he worse than a home invader who rapes, kills, and robs the occupant of the home? All of the aforementioned crimes have happened, yet none have been classed as a hate crime. The perpetrators of those crimes will get lighter sentences than a person who commits a so-called hate crime.

The idea of hate crimes, as fostered by the PC movement, is irrational and totally lacking in common sense.

~~*~~

The PC Movement and Racism

The favorite weapon of the PC movement is the race card. The race card can be played in almost any given circumstance. Facts can be twisted, distorted or mutilated in any way to make it appear that racism is involved.

To disagree with our president is racist. To oppose welfare is racist. Even to suggest that welfare recipients should verify that they qualify for welfare is racist. According to Liberals, forcing welfare recipients to prove they need welfare is degrading. If that is so, wouldn't the mere act of applying for welfare be degrading?

Or wouldn't it be even more degrading to fraudulently draw welfare?

Many poor people who actually need welfare often complain of seeing welfare claimants in the welfare office driving expensive cars and wearing expensive jewelry and clothes. Customers at checkout lines commonly point out that people use food stamps to buy expensive items. Many non-food stamp customers cannot afford such items, and even must resort to cutting corners by buying store brands. Some must forego buying even some of the store brands.

Most people agree that if they had to go on welfare they would not mind in the least showing proof that they need it.

According to Liberals, to agree that we should show an ID to vote is racist because showing an ID would block many minorities from voting. The PC crowd has been saying that for so long that they actually believe it. How can it be racist to show ID to vote? People of color, just like everyone else, must show an ID to buy whiskey or for any number of things. They must get a license to drive...and the license itself becomes an ID. The vast majority of minorities drive cars and large numbers of them buy alcoholic beverages...just as white people do.

~~*~~

If a waitress gives poor service to a white person she's a bad waitress, but if she gives poor service to a Black person the PC movement says she's a racist. Many brainwashed Blacks simply do not understand that when a waiter, sales person, cashier, mechanic, or any person who serves the public, is rude to them, there is a ninety percent chance that the person is rude to everyone.

Many reasons come into play that will make a person rude to others, a fight with a spouse, a hangover, or a number of other reasons. But some Blacks have become so brainwashed and sensitized by the PC movement that they will cry racism at the slightest hint of rudeness.

Many, many Whites have stood at service desks in stores and been ignored, almost as if they're invisible...and many get upset and angry. Many Blacks also get upset at being ignored, but some are so thin skinned due to PC brainwashing that they believe they're ignored because of their skin color.

Our president once said that black men hear locks on cars clicking as they go by. In these days and times anyone who doesn't lock their car doors is foolish. I lock mine every time I get out, and many times there will be black men nearby. I don't doubt that some people might not lock their car if Blacks are around, just to show they trust black people. It really doesn't matter who is around, anyone who doesn't lock their car doors is foolish.

So, the PC movement would have us think that white people who lock their car doors when Blacks are present are racist. Good grief.

The PC movement is working on other nonwhites, too. A Japanese friend once confided that he was waiting at a bus stop one chilly morning when one of the Whites remarked, "It's a bit nippy out this morning." Thinking the man was playing on words because he, a "Nip" was among the group, he gave the man a dirty look. The man looked confused. The Japanese-American came to realize later that the man was probably just making a common statement

29

that many would make on a chilly morning. The PC movement works to divide us.

A Native American woman defaced the 9/11 memorial because she was brainwashed into hating white people, and believed it to be a memorial to white people. Of course it isn't. It is a memorial to all the 3,000 plus victims, which included just about every race, religion, and nationality.

~~*~~

The Goofy PC Movement

As has already been mentioned, it is just plain goofy to punish a six year old boy for kissing a six year old girl. (We might wonder if the kids had both been of the same sex whether it would have been permissible.)   And of course kids pointing their fingers and shouting "bang" is a no no. And sketching the likeness of a pistol is taboo.

But what could be more silly than taking "man" out of words and replacing it with "person." Now we have clumsy words like journeyperson, helmsperson and lineperson. Or how about the way we use "man" to mean the whole human race. It's no longer correct to say things like "manmade," or "since the dawn of mankind."

But the height of silliness by the PC movement is its opposition to the names of sports teams, high school. college, and pro. Most of the Native American Indians paid absolutely no attention to teams with names of their tribes or nations. But like Blacks and other minorities, the brainwashing eventually got to them. So where a Native American never even noticed that a football team was named after his people...or he might actually have been proud of it...he now found himself demonstrating against the team.

Some Native Americans, though, actually are proud of teams bearing their names. When some Native Americans against tribal names of sports teams demanded that the Florida State Seminoles change their name, the Seminole people themselves stepped in and said that they approved of the team name, and that they were proud of it. Hooray for a little sanity.

But it was a small setback for the PC movement. Their gains have been far, far more impressive.

More silliness by the PC movement: Sambo's Restaurant was forced to change its name because the PC police thought the name "Sambo" would be associated with the children's story, "Little Black Sambo." Actually the name was derived from parts of the names of the owners, <u>Sam</u> Battistone and Newell <u>Boh</u>nett.

But anyway, what's the big deal if the restaurant *were* named after the character in the story. That would be up to the author of the story to sue the restaurant owners...if he/she chose to do so. Blacks, just like everyone else, have the right to sue if they have a grievance against anyone.

There are some who consider peanut butter and jelly sandwiches as offensive to Hispanic children because that food is not part of their culture.

The PC police in Oregon have decided that there should be no mention of brown bagging, as the color of brown bags was once used as a standard for skin color to determine the status a person. That was many years ago. It would be interesting if such a standard was applied in places like South Florida, where there are large numbers of Caucasian people with deep tans.

~~*~~

The PC Movement and American Exceptionalism

Almost from the start of her existence, America has been a beacon of opportunity and liberty to the world. Many countries around the world have emulated America, adopting democratic forms of governments or republics.

Millions of immigrants have flocked to our shores seeking the freedom and opportunities in this country. Why on Earth would we want to change our government that has been a beacon of freedom to the world? Admittedly, there have been blots in our history. The shameful institution of slavery was with us when the nation was born and lasted until the Emancipation Proclamation. In WWII people of Japanese ancestry were shamefully interned in concentration camps and held there until the war's end.

31

Many of those Americans of Japanese ancestry are still living among us today. Those who lived in the camps during those shameful times have been paid restitution, and though they must have bitter memories, they have once again integrated into American society and become good citizens. As a note of interest, while the Japanese Americans were being held in those concentration camps, large numbers of Japanese Americans from Hawaii volunteered for the U.S. Army. The army formed them into the 442nd Regimental Combat Team. *The 442nd Regimental Combat Team became the most highly decorated American unit of World War II.*

Slavery has been abolished for one hundred and fifty years. After the Civil War, Jim crow laws followed in the southern states. Those disgraceful laws have been abolished for a half century. Since the abolishment of Jim Crow Laws, there has been no institutional racism. What racism has remained is individual racism, and is still around today. It most probably always will be.

Individual racists cannot be arrested and punished merely for hating someone of another race, just as no one can be arrested for hating Jews, Catholics, Japanese, Germans, or any other specific group (not yet, anyway.) If, however, a racist breaks a law by burning a church, assaulting others, or otherwise harming others because of their race, he would be subject to arrest and punishment.

One convicted of a hate crime not only pays the penalty for the crime he committed, but the thought behind that crime. A giant leap toward thought control.

Recently there has been talk of bringing "hope and change" to America. The PC movement is firmly behind this movement to bring about change. It fits in perfectly with Marxist plans to change this country.

To want to bring change to the one nation that has long been the leader of the free nations of the world is folly. Of course America is not perfect, and change in some areas would serve to improve the country. But the change advocated by the Marxist PC movement can bring nothing but disaster. And disaster is on the way if we don't stop it.

Marxism and Liberalism

The Liberal agenda plays right into the hands of the Marxists, who take a Liberal idea and modify it to fit their more radical agenda. They then establish it as a politically correct concept and it becomes taboo to speak out against it. But a number of people will speak out. They will pay the price...and stir up resentment among conservatives and the more moderate Independents. Divide and conquer.

The PC movement has invaded nearly every facet of our lives. Politics, religion, race, sex, the workplace, schools, you name it. We're divided as never before: men vs. women, religion vs. religion, Liberals vs. Conservatives, ethnic groups vs. ethnic groups, and political parties vs. political parties. There's always been some friction between some of these factions, but not nearly to the extent as it is today. Just monitor Liberal forums and Conservative forums on the internet and you can feel the venomous hatred in their comments.

Even global warming has been invaded by the PC movement. To be politically correct, you must profess to believe that global warming is caused by man. To profess to believe that it is occurring naturally is taboo.

Coal, one of America's greatest natural resources, is under attack by the PC environmentalists. Coal is a major source of our energy, and its by products supply us with many of our needs. In addition, the coal industry provides us with thousands of jobs. Is it any wonder that the industry is under attack by the Marxist PC movement? Just another attempt to weaken us.

We burden American industry with heavy environmental regulations, so industry, in order to stay solvent, outsources their manufacturing to China. China then manufactures the products using cheap coal as fuel. Any pollution they create will of course find its way around the world, including the U.S. But this is fine with the PC Marxists, they have found another way to weaken our country

Because of PC we're afraid to open our mouths. We're afraid to express our opinions. We're afraid to criticize any group. We're sometimes even afraid to tell the truth. And now we're afraid to criticize our president. This is the Land of the Free? Anyone who thinks this is still the land of the free hasn't been paying attention.

~~*~~

The PC movement and Immigration.

Every country has immigration laws. Whether strict or lax, countries need to keep some sort of control over those who enter its borders. The immigration laws of the United States can definitely be counted among the most lax. Our borders are also among the least secure when compared to other countries...such as Mexico. Because of this, we have millions of illegal immigrants within our borders and more flowing in every day.

The PC movement has decreed that Illegal Immigrant is to be another taboo word. We're now supposed to call them undocumented immigrants. That makes about as much sense as saying a bank robber made an undocumented withdrawal.

Contrary to the brainwashing of legal immigrants, most Americans have always seen Hispanic-Americans as fellow Americans...and still do, although some may be turned off by the brainwashed Legals supporting the Illegals. Divide and conquer.

~~*~~

We Can Turn It Around

Younger Americans don't realize what is happening. They were born into an America with political correctness in full swing. They don't know what rights and freedoms have been lost because they have never experienced those rights and freedoms. For that matter, many older Americans don't realize what is happening because the Marxist movement has crept so slowly and subtly into our society it has gone unnoticed.

But what can we do about it? Plenty, but we must be as motivated, tenacious, and energetic as the PC crowd. Here are some suggestions:

1.) Watch your representatives closely, including those in federal, state, county, and municipal governments. Watch how they vote, what they do and what they support, not what they say. They depend on us to have short memories. No matter how terrible the job they have done, at election time they tell us how great they were. Keep a written record of how they vote. It's fairly easy to get their voting record on the internet, and local newspapers usually tell how they vote.

Note down what they have promised, and check your notes at reelection time. Too many people simply forget what politicians, including presidents, promise. Keep notes and check your notes.

Remember: They depend on you to have a short memory.

The absolute best way to stop the politicians who are influenced by the PC movement is to vote them out.

2.) Anticipate that public school teachers will brainwash your child by teaching them such things as that all white settlers in America were evil, and by extension we, their descendants are also evil. They teach that Capitalism is evil, and that Socialism is good. You have the advantage in that you have the child with you from his/her earliest years, so prepare them for the brainwashing.

Prepare your children to resist the brainwashing all through the school years, and especially in college. Keep reminding them of the good things about America. Don't "force feed" them, just be matter of fact. Remind your children that they may be taught negative things about America. Also remind them not to argue with teachers, but to simply ignore the negative things some teachers may say.

3.) *Be active in the PTA whenever you can.* Try to get on school boards if you can. Sit in on classes whenever you can.

Check out text books, as some of them have been found to contain anti-American or pro-Marxist propaganda.

4.)   If you find that your public school is teaching history, literature--and ***even math problems*** that are infused with anti-American propaganda, try to enroll your children in a good private school if you possibly can.   Perhaps people can join together as groups and pool their resources in setting up a school.

5.)   Write, email, or phone your elected representatives often, and each time they are supporting an injustice caused by the PC movement.

6.)   Boycott businesses that fire or punish their employees because they have dared to break the rules of the PC movement. Be active, urge friends, relatives, and neighbors to join in boycotts. Go out of your way to give your business to stores, restaurants, and other businesses that fight the PC movement, such as Chick-Fil-A.

7.)   Start anti-PC organizations to protest and demonstrate against laws that favor the PC movement and suppress those who disagree with it.

8.) Companies, news media, industry, and local government are on the PC bandwagon. They are afraid to do or say anything that might offend some PC protected group. Make them afraid of you. Write them, call them, email them, and mention them on Facebook or Twitter. Ask your family, friends, and acquaintances to do likewise. Now is the time; this PC disease has already infected too many. Start resisting them today.

Be ready to fight the PC movement anywhere you find it. Our representatives in congress, our supreme court, and even our president have done nothing to curb this oppressive movement, so we must be prepared to unite and fight for our freedom.   Our greatest weapon is our vote. ***Our greatest weapon is our vote.*** Be on the lookout for politicians who support PC legislation.

Keep in mind that Political Correctness is not merely a pesky nuisance, but a ***tool of Marxism*** out to establish their brand of socialism in America. Even now it is conditioning our minds into accepting their oppressive ways.

We are now being told by the PC movement what we can and cannot do to celebrate Christmas. We must forsake Christmas traditions that we have enjoyed for over a century. We are now being told what religious symbols we can and cannot display. We are now being told what choices of words we may or may not use to designate or describe certain groups or activities.

The PC movement says that you must be ashamed of being white. To admit that you are not ashamed of being white, straight, or Christian immediately brands you as a racist, homophobe, or Islamaphobe.

It has been decided for us what programs we can or cannot see on TV. Censors are busy cutting out "offensive" parts of old movies, which were made during times when we had more freedom.

Look for and support leaders who can lead us out of this PC morass. There are two kinds of leaders we need to avoid. The first is the politician that merely says what you want to hear. Pay attention to their words, yes, but also pay attention to their voting records.

The second to avoid is the bigot and racist. The PC movement will be loudly screaming "racist" and "bigot" at any who dare to oppose them and their m. Having leaders who are racists and bigots will simply give the PC movement the appearance of credibility. We don't need that.

It will be a struggle to fight the PC movement because it has become so firmly entrenched in our society. But it can be done. The majority of Americans oppose it, but no one up to now has started a really serious movement against it. It's time to start a movement, for if we delay too long we will find ourselves under the heels of jack booted oppressors.

Almost everybody fears the PC police now, even police departments, the Army, Navy, Air Force and Marines of the United States. Some army officers had reason to suspect that Major Hassan, a Muslim, was a security risk, but kept their mouths shut for fear of being booted out of the army because they would be labeled as Islamophobes. This is just one example of what political correctness is doing to us.

By following the above listed proposals we can possibly turn our country away from the ruinous ways of the PC movement. But we would have to follow the proposals stringently and resolutely, for the Marxists of the PC M have been digging in for years. They have duped large numbers of Americans into believing that political correctness is a good thing.

The harm to our nation and our way of life given here is just the tip of the ice berg. Every day that passes we can see or hear in the news of more ridiculous but harmful incidents incited by the PC movement. Many of these incidents are brought about by intelligent, well educated people...who are totally lacking in plain old common sense. One of the greatest boons to the Marxists is the teachers, professors, administrators, and politicians who display their lack of common sense by enforcing the noxious rules of the PC movement.

~~*~~

We can keep things the way they are and accept the changes that are eroding our freedom, or we can emulate The Greatest Generation and fight the evil forces trying to destroy our country and our way of life. The PC movement may be a bigger threat to our freedom than Nazi Germany or Soviet Russia.

Our greatest weapon is our vote, friends, our greatest weapon is our vote.

End

~~*~~

About the Author

Donald H Sullivan is a native of St. Augustine, Florida, presently living in NC. He started his writing career shortly after retirement from the U.S. Army. He welcomes comments about this book or about any of the other books he has written.

His twenty year army career included service with The Corps of Engineers, Air Defense Artillery, Military Intelligence, and

Psychological Operations.

He began his writing career in the army when one of his assignments included writing tech manuals. Pretty dry stuff, but it whetted his appetite for writing.

Politically, he could be described as an Eisenhower Centrist. He is a registered Democrat, but considers himself an Independent, leaning sometimes to the right and sometimes to the left.

He loves animals, especially dogs.

He can be reached by e-mail at: dhsully@gmail.com

His official website: dhsully.wix.com/part1

Following is a story from Sullivan's book, "Tales of Suspense and Mystery"

Secrets of a Psycho
By Donald H Sullivan

Alfred Jenkins was on his way home from his wife's funeral. He looked at the passenger seat and began to chuckle. "I wonder if your ghost is sitting there, Irene. Are you watching my driving, angry because you have no voice to nag me now?" He was laughing aloud now, so hard that he was banging his hands against the steering wheel.

"Y'know. I had to grit my teeth to keep from laughing and dancing at your funeral. I wanted to bust out singing 'Good Night Irene." I did giggle through my handkerchief, but they thought I was crying."

He stopped for a red light, still laughing. He looked around and saw that the woman in the car next to his was staring at him.

Stupid bitch. What the hell is she staring at. If I pulled my switchblade and waved it at her she would have something to stare at. Hey, how would she like it if I cut her damn throat.

He looked at her and smiled. "Something funny I heard on the radio," he said. She nodded and smiled.

The light changed and he continued. "Oh, it's so funny, Irene. They think you fell from the step ladder while changing a light bulb. Only you and I know the truth. Oh, I know you disapprove of my putting you out of your misery. But there ain't a damn thing you can do about it 'cause you're just a spirit now.

"No body, no voice, no nothing. Just your spirit. Now all you can do is just sit there and behave yourself." He burst into a fit of laughter. "Betcha wish that you could do me some mischief."

Hey, that reminds me. I got a couple of secrets that nobody knows but me, and now I'm gonna share them with you."

~~*~~

He pulled into the driveway of the small frame house. "You always complained about. this little house, Irene. Only two bedrooms wasn't enough for you? Look, we never had any kids, so what did we need another room for? Well, it don't matter to you now, does it?"

"Hey, looky there, Irene. Our lawn is mowed, probably the airhead slut next door. And looks like she watered the ugly flowers that you planted. Damn busybody. But don't you worry, she'll soon be outta her misery. Like you." He playfully punched the "spirit" in the passenger's seat. "Ain't ya glad, Sweetie?"

He entered the house, and after locking the door behind him, he jumped up on the couch. He began jumping up and down on the couch like a child, all the while whooping with laughter. He jumped down and started dancing, and then fell rolling on the floor.

The doorbell rang. He jumped up, straightened his clothes, and went to the door. It was Michelle Fletcher from next door. She was carrying a covered tray. "Hi Mr. Jenkins. Mom and I are so sorry we couldn't make it to the funeral, but you know, Mom was feeling ill, and her being in a wheelchair and all. Anyway, we brought you a little something. There's roast chicken and the trimmings."

"I understand," he said, "and thanks for the food. I really appreciate it. And I want to thank you for mowing my lawn and taking care of Irene's prized flowers. You are so kind, and I'm really grateful."

"I'm glad to be of help in any way I can, Mr. Jenkins. I'd like to say once more that if there is anything we can do, just let us know." She gave him a hug and left.

"You see that, Irene? That gal's got the hots for me. Oh boy, she rubbed them little boobs against me. And wow, them skimpy white shorts she was wearing, showing off them sexy legs. Wheee! Wanted to give me a show with those legs and the firm little boobies.. So she ain't even half my age, but who cares? Well, anyways, one of the secrets I'm gonna tell you is how I'm gonna put little Miss Boobie and her stupid wheelchair mom out of their misery."

He turned on the TV, placed the tray with the chicken on the coffee table, then sat down to watch a rerun of *The Andy Griffith Show*.

"Yummy, this chicken's good. Wanna piece? Oops, I forgot, you can't eat it. Well, I'll eat it for you. Hey, I almost forgot about the secrets. I'm gonna take you out into the hills tonight and show you one of 'em. Something real nice. You'll love it"

~~*~~

After nightfall, Alfred left the house and drove out of town. About a mile out of town, he turned off on an unpaved, winding gravel road leading into hilly country. "You never been out here before, Irene. This is part of my rural mail route. Know it like the back of my hand."

Presently he stopped and got out of the car. The full moon made the night almost as bright as daylight. "See that hill? Just follow me and I'll show you something. He trudged about halfway up the hill and stopped near a large boulder protruding from the ground.

"Just a few paces from the left of that boulder there's two graves, and in those graves lies two lovely girls." He giggled and danced a little jig. "Couple of real lookers, too. Whee! Now didn't I tell you you'd love it? See, now you got company, ain't that nice? Irene, this here is Candice and Barbara." He did a little bow and gestured toward the graves.

"Course you do remember the girls being in the news? One about three years back and the other just last summer. Seems they disappeared and was never found." He giggled. "Lovers come up here and park sometimes, but who'd ever guess what's here? But I keep a map of the place and an account of what happened to the girls, because I'm gonna be famous after I'm gone. I keep it in that little gray strongbox that you always thought was where I kept important papers and records of my mail deliveries. Well, now ya know."

He took a deep breath, and his mood seemed to grow melancholy. "The girls was hitchhikers just passing through and I picked 'em up in the mail truck. I put 'em out of their misery just like I did for you. Used a different method, though. Sliced 'em up with my switchblade."

He walked a little way farther up the hill, about ten paces past the boulder. "Maria Sanchez is where I'm standing, and about three paces farther up is Connie Barker. I put them out of their misery with my blade. You probably don't remember Maria. She was an itinerate fruit picker." He laughed until he was gasping. "Oh, she was so easy. I promised her twenty bucks to help me deliver my mail, and the stupid bitch believed me."

He pointed to the other grave. "Connie loved her booze. She was drunk, and was staggering to the liquor store to get more whiskey when I picked her up and gave her a lift."

Tears were streaming down his cheeks now. "It gets so lonesome up here, and they are always so glad to see me." A smile came to his face. "Look, Irene, they have risen from their graves to dance for me." He clapped his hands. "Yay...that's wonderful girls. I love ya." He threw kisses toward the graves.

"I promised them that I would bring more girls up here to keep them company. And I will, too."

He got back in the car and started back toward town. He looked in the back seat. "Nobody there. Well, looks like your new friends don't want to go back with us. They never leave the hill. Like it there, I guess. But don't feel bad, 'cause we'll come back to see 'em. I sometimes stop by to visit while I'm driving the mail truck on my route. If anybody sees me they figure I'm just taking a pee."

~~*~~

Soon after leaving the gravel road and turning onto the paved road, he noticed a pair of headlights pull up behind him. He didn't like the glare of lights behind him at night. He cursed, then slowed down a little to let the other car pass. But it didn't.

"Now why the hell don't that idiot pass. The road is clear and he has all the room in the world."

He slowed down a little more, but the car stayed with him. He was considering pulling over to let the other driver pass when he saw flashing blue lights in his rear view mirror.

"Damn, a cop. Out of the city limits, so probably a state trooper. Now what could I have been doing? Does he know something?" He glanced at his speedometer. Under the speed limit. He never exceeded the speed limit so he knew that wasn't the reason.

He fingered the switchblade in his pocket. "If he tries to arrest me, I'll get close enough to stick this into his stupid heart. I'll leave him here and nobody will know what happened."

He pulled over and waited. A moment later the trooper appeared.

"Your driver's license, please sir?"

He fished the license out and handed it to the trooper. The trooper studied it a moment and handed it back to him.

"Mr. Jenkins, I just want to tell you that you have a burned out tail light on your right rear. I won't write you up, but I would advise that you get it fixed as soon as possible."

"Thank you very much, Officer. I certainly will take care of it."

~~*~~

The following morning was Sunday and Alfred slept late. He crawled out of bed, went to the bathroom, and then went to the kitchen. He made coffee and filled a bowl with frosted flakes. He looked across the table as he ate. "Ha, thought I couldn't make my own breakfast, didn't ya. Well, I can make it by myself, Dearie, and do lots of other things. You'll see."

It was after 10:AM when he finished breakfast. He got up from the table and immediately went to the window in the living room. He lifted a slat in the blinds and peered through the crack just in time to see Michelle spreading a blanket in her back yard. She was wearing shorts with orange and white vertical stripes.

She spread the blanket and turned on her portable radio. "Whee! Just look at that, Irene. That girl's putting on another show for me. She's just begging for it. Wants to join you, Barbara, Maria, Connie, and Candice. And you know what, Dearie? It gets better each time I do it. Bashing your head was fun, but the switchblade is better."

He watched as Mrs. Fletcher wheeled out to join her daughter, and moments later a young man joined the two women.

"Ha. That idiot of a boyfriend is there again. What does she see in that moron?"

He closed the crack in the blind and reached into his pocket, drawing out an eight-inch switchblade.

He pressed the button and the blade made a click as it sprang open. He felt the razor sharp edge, thinking of the red gash one stroke of its thin bright blade would make on Michelle's throat. "Oh the pleasure," he said, "the ecstasy." He felt a stirring in his groin as his finger touched the razor-sharp edge.

"I'm gonna let you in on the other secret, Dearie. Remember when Michelle and her mother were gone for two weeks and left their house keys with us? Well guess what, I secretly had copies of the keys made for their security storm door and the standard door at the front entrance." He peeked through the blinds again. "I know where your bedroom is, my Michelle." He then sang out in a hoarse, tuneless voice, "Michelle ma belle," then stopped and went into a fit of giggling until he lay on the floor gasping. "Yep, tonight's gonna be the night."

He watched their backyard picnic until they went back indoors and then watched Michelle's boyfriend leave.

You won't have her tomorrow, you stupid turd. She'll be mine.

~~*~~

Alfred finished his supper, went into the living room, and

44

turned on the TV. "We'll stay here and watch TV until they go to bed," he said. "Michelle don't go to bed until after 11:00, so I'll give her plenty of time to go to sleep. It'll be so easy. No dog or no alarm system. They think the barred windows and barred security doors are enough." He tapped his temple with his forefinger. "But not enough for a smart and cunning man like me."

"I'm gonna do this by myself, Irene. I want this to be just me and Michelle. I'll have to take her mother, too." He laughed. "I'll let you participate in taking out her mother. But when I take Michelle, it will just be me and her."

He went into a pensive mood. "You know, Irene, they are always terrified when I put them out of their misery, but they are always so thrilled and happy afterwards. All except you. You seem to be the only one that wasn't happy to go." He made mocking boo hoo sounds. "Well that's just too bad, Sweet."

~~*~~

He continued to watch TV, getting up periodically to peer out the window at the Fletcher's house.

"Would you look at that, Irene? It's 11:30 and their lights are still on. They must be watching a movie or something. That's OK. I can wait. Let the whores enjoy themselves while they can. They won't watch anything after tonight."

But he became impatient. He turned off his TV and stationed himself at the window. He saw the lights go on in Mrs. Fletcher's bedroom, and then darken at 11:50. But the living room lights stayed on.

"The old witch has gone to bed, so my Michelle should be going to her room soon. "He giggled. "Wish they'd leave their blinds open. It'd be nice if she gave me one last show tonight. I'm kinda disappointed. But I suppose you're gloating about that, Irene. You always seem to like anything that disappoints me."

He watched the living room lights go out at 12:30. Michelle's bedroom lights came on a moment later. Five minutes later her lights went out.

"Finally. It won't be long now, My Belle. You'll be out of your misery soon."

He reached in his pocket and grasped his switchblade. He shivered, and felt a stirring in his groin.

~~*~~

Alfred left the house shortly before 2:00 AM. Making sure that there were no cars coming from either direction, he kept in the shadows and used shrubbery for cover as he stealthily made his way to the Fletcher's house. He stepped up onto the stoop and quietly inserted the key into the barred storm door. There was a slight squeak as he pulled the door open.

The second door opened noiselessly. He pulled off his loafers before entering. Using a small flashlight, he made his way through the living room, and then into the hallway. He passed the bedroom of Michelle's mother. He saw her form on the bed and almost giggled when he heard her snoring.

He made his way to Michelle's bedroom door. Her door was also open. He crept to her bedside, and stood there looking down at her. He would awaken her an instant before pulling the blade across her neck. It was important that she would know her fate, and that he, Alfred Jenkins, was giving her relief, putting an end to her misery.

He pulled the switchblade from his pocket, and opened it with a soft click. She moaned softly and turned facing toward the wall. It presented no problem for him, for her throat was still exposed. As he held the knife near her throat, a feeling of such euphoria came over him that he had to control his shaking. He now had the ultimate power over another human being; the power of life and death.

As he gazed down at her, exulting over his power, he caught a slight movement in the corner of the room. He looked to see a dark, shadowy figure standing there. As he stared at the figure, two glowing eyes formed, looking directly at him. He gasped, and Michelle stirred again.

Never taking its glowing eyes off of him, the figure advanced.

"Irene," he yelled, "you can't do this. No, no, you think you're gonna scare me but you can't."

Michelle screamed and jumped from her bed. But as her feet hit

46

the floor and she started to run, her foot got caught in the sheets and she fell forward. Her head hit the floor and she was still.

The figure kept advancing. "No! Go away. You're a spirit and you can't hurt me. You're not scaring me, Irene. Keep away or I'll kill you again."

As the figure neared, he swiped at it with the knife. The knife went harmlessly through the air, but the figure disappeared.

"I warned you, Irene."

He turned his attention back to Michelle, who was lying still on the floor. She moaned. He approached her and grabbed a handful of her hair. She tried to pull away, but he yanked her head back exposing her throat. But as he moved the switchblade toward her throat, he saw the shadowy figure again, this time joined by four more shadows.

"Go away, all of you. I'll kill everyone of you again. And you won't stop me from taking my lovely Michelle."

He reached down again with the switchblade. But he hesitated when heard a noise behind him. The lights went on and the shadowy figures disappeared. At that moment he came to the realization that the figures weren't real, but only existed in his mind.

He spun around to see Mrs. Fletcher in her wheelchair in the doorway.

"Damn you. Damn you. I'll kill you for this. You've spoiled everything, you bitch."

He ran at her with the knife, but as he did, he saw something in her hand. There was a roar and Alfred felt as if he'd been punched in the chest. He looked down, his mouth opened in surprise and shock, to see blood pumping from the wound.

Another roar was the last sound Alfred Jenkins ever heard.

The End

Books by Donald H Sullivan:

Our Canine Companions: Featuring Whiskers
Tales of Wonder
Project Genesis
Tales of Suspense and Mystery
Terrific Tales of Sci-fi and Space Opera
Whiskers
Chillers
Taino
Boriken
The Magical Earth
Three Amazing Tales
The Psionic Man
Turnbull's Slaves: A Minorcan Story
Intruder
Werewolf of Misty Valley
Turnbull's Slaves: A Minorcan Story, Plus Taino

~~*~~

www.ingramcontent.com/pod-product-compliance
Lightning Source LLC
Chambersburg PA
CBHW050347290526
45785CB00006B/2667